Thanksgiving

Adult Coloring Book

CREATIVE COLORING PRESS

First edition: 2016

Disclaimer/Limit of Liability
This book is for informational purposes only. The views expressed are those of the author alone, and should not be taken as expert, legal, or medical advice. The reader is responsible for his or her own actions.

Photo credits: Shutterstock

HAPPY
THANKSGIVING

HAPPY
THANKSGIVING
FAMILY

Happy Thanksgiving

Autumn

HAPPY
THANKS
GIVING
DAY!

35898415R00039

Made in the USA
Middletown, DE
18 October 2016